Original title: The Secrets We Write

Author: Liina Liblikas
Editor: Jessica Elisabeth Luik
ISBN 978-9916-39-464-9

The Secrets We Write

Liina Liblikas

Serenades of the Sealed

In silence, whispers break the stone,
A chorus sealed in earth and bone.
The shadows dance to a tune unheard,
Echoes of a song unstirred.

Secrets hum in cryptic chords,
Harmonies trapped, without words.
Each hush a verse, a serenade sealed,
In the quiet, their power revealed.

Muted aria, soft and deep,
Where sealed serenades gently weep.
Beneath the ground, their melody spills,
A cadence bound by silent wills.

Arcana of Affection Penned

Script the love in cryptic lines,
The fervor hidden, neatly scribed.
A parchment full of veiled signs,
With strokes where passion is imbued.

The ink runs deep, a mystic hue,
An arcana of the tender view.
Emotions etched with careful hands,
In symbols only hearts understand.

Encoded whispers through the quill,
A craft of love, an artful skill.
Each letter blooms, a hidden flower,
Penned affection's secret power.

Undercurrents of Utterance

Unspoken truths that ebb and flow,
Like rivers beneath a calm veneer.
In depths where silent undercurrents grow,
There lie the words we do not hear.

A gaze, a pause, a touch so slight,
Convey the tales we dare not speak.
The nuances of the dimmest light,
Translate the essence of the meek.

In gestures small, the story told,
Sights and whispers softly meet.
The currents carry, bold yet cold,
The utterance of the incomplete.

Dialogues of the Veiled Heart

In the chamber of the veiled heart,
Dialogues are silent, set apart.
A murmur wrapped in secrecy,
A dance of shadows, you and me.

Whispered words in the theatre of mime,
A pantomime of feelings sublime.
Each motion speaks, though lips stand still,
A conversation without the shrill.

Behind the curtain of the chest,
Where beats are heard, and thoughts are pressed.
The veiled heart speaks in pantomime,
An endless dialogue, through the sands of time.

Mandalas of My Silence

In the quiet sphere where thoughts collide,
Yet in their echo, my whisper resides.
A mandala forms, in silence it spins,
Each curve and line my spirit inscribes.

Ephemeral circles, loop without end,
In the void's embrace, they gently extend.
My muted palette, of dreams they consist,
Silhouettes of solace, to the cosmos I send.

Layered in the stillness, my secrets unfold,
In intricate patterns, my stories are told.
A silent symphony, in the air it hangs,
In the fabric of silence, my world I mold.

Each mandala's spin, a quiet confession,
In tranquil revolutions, lies my expression.
A sacred geometry, in hush it is traced,
In the mandalas of silence, I find my essence.

Codex of the Covert Heart

Beneath the guarded chest of flesh,
Lies the cryptic codex, emotions mesh.
Writ in the ink of pulsing streams,
A compendium of whispered dreams.

Turn the page, a silent beat,
In every throb, two souls greet.
A covert heart, in rhythm locked,
Behind ribbed walls, gently rocked.

Scripted in the chambers deep,
Are the secrets that I keep.
In every pulse, an encrypted art,
A language formed within my heart.

The codex holds, in vessels wove,
The silent tales of hidden love.
In every line, a clandestine part,
Within the codex of the covert heart.

Inscriptions of Invisible Walls

Unseen marks upon the air,
Borders felt that aren't quite there.
Invisible walls, in silence raised,
Within their bounds, my spirit's phased.

On these barriers, time engraves,
Scribbles of moments, in shadows it saves.
Transient words, no eyes behold,
Narratives brave and tales untold.

Scripts of the silent, etchings of the blind,
Encrypted scribbles, that only I find.
Inscriptions felt, on walls unseen,
My mind's graffiti, on surfaces clean.

Each wall a chapter, in quiet spelled,
Inaudible tales, in restraint held.
On plastered silence, my musings sprawl,
In the inscriptions of invisible walls.

Muted Testimonies Drafted

In silent halls of whispered past,
A tale of woe and bravery vast.
Echoes lost to time's cold grasp,
Muted testimonies, in velvet clasp.

Tattered pages bound by fealty,
Harken to the voice of reality.
Though the spirits of lore are daunted,
Their silent vigils remain undaunted.

Within the shadows, truths are sequestered,
By ageless ink, their fates are mastered.
History's fabric, finely crafted,
In muted testimonies, forever drafted.

Masked Tales Jotted

Behind masquerades of ink and quill,
Stories dance, some bitter, some trill.
Veiling truth in guises begotten,
Variant tints of masked tales jotted.

Words pirouette on parchment sheer,
Each a mask, eluding fear.
Lines intertwine in secret plot,
Narratives veiled, ever to be sought.

In mystery's script, the heart conspires,
Fingers scribe with silent fires.
Through cloaks of allegory they trot,
In the silent saga of tales jotted.

Obscure Lore Etched

Upon the stone, time's hand has sketched,
Figures and runes, in mystery drenched.
Scriptures of a forgotten epoch,
Stories hidden, as if by lock.

In shadows, grooves tell a silent tale,
The narrative of a storm-swept gale.
Carved by a hand, both rough and steady,
Obscure lore upon the rock, so weighty.

Whispers of ancients, in lines embedded,
A chronicle that nature has credited.
Lingering thoughts, both bold and fetched,
In the permanence of lore etched.

Hushed Words Weaved

Through the tapestry of hushed reprieve,
Words intertwine, magic they conceive.
Softly spun tales of silken thread,
Weaving patterns, where secrets tread.

The warp and weft of whispered song,
Narratives gentle, yet strikingly strong.
In the loom of silence, they're interlaced,
Hushed words in complex patterns graced.

Quietly arrayed in rows unseen,
Stitched with echoes of what has been.
Gentle passage of hand over weaved seam,
In the muted beauty of a dreamer’s dream.

Confessions to a Diary

Secret whispers in the fold
Hidden truths yet to be told
Ink flows deep on pages bare
Silent witness to the share

Each day etched with silent script
Emotions in confinement dipped
Fear and hope in a tight dance
Diary holds a life's expanse

Leather-bound, my confidante
With every stroke, a whispered want
Through lines, my soul begins to sigh
Within these pages, thoughts don't die

Burden lightened with each word
Unseen, unheard, but always heard
In you, my deepest self I confide
Within you, my secrets abide

Chronicles of Silence

In the quiet, words unspoken
Lie the chronicles, unbroken
Whispers of what could have been
Lost in silence, left unseen

Time moves forth without a trace
Stillness fills the empty space
Echoes of the unsaid wait
In the void, they resonate

Mute testimony to the past
Silent moments meant to last
Ghosts of words, they haunt the air
In the hush, their tales they share

Hiding in a soundless void
All the stories unenjoyed
Chronicle the silence deep
Where unuttered secrets keep

Prose of the Concealed

Whispered lines of hidden lore
Behind the mind's secretive door
Words wrapped in enigma's veil
In this prose, the truths entail

Shadowed tales of days untold
Written in a code so bold
Curtains draped so none can see
What lies beneath, what yearns to be

Within the dusk of thought's domain
Lies a world that's not the same
Elusive essence captured tight
In words that dance away from light

Ever veiled, the inner eye
Conceals its gaze from open sky
Here I pen the concealed verse
Where meaning hides within the terse

Encrypted in Rhyme

Beneath the rhythm, beneath the time
Lies a message, encrypted in rhyme
Verses hold keys to a secret door
Where meaning hides, forevermore

Each stanza, a lock of intricate make
Requires wit's hand the code to break
Words align in harmonious chime
To shield a truth, to guard a prime

Read between lines of meter, of beat
Find the pulse, the hidden feat
In the poem's heart, the essence climbs
Revealed to those who see the signs

For those who listen, a revelation
An enigma's end, a found foundation
Encrypted in rhyme, a knowledge fine
In every line, a cipher divine

Incognito Narratives Elaborated

Whispered secrets under the moon's gaze,
Hidden stories wrapped in the night's haze,
Arcane whispers in the air, barely heard,
Enigmatic tales unfold, word by word.

In shadows move the bearers of the lore,
Incognito, they keep the ancient core,
Narratives veiled, weaving through the time,
Revealed only to those who seek the sublime.

Silhouettes dance with every story spun,
Cryptic is the language they've begun,
Each masquerading a truth untold,
In the darkness, their narratives bold.

Shadowed Haikus Formed

Night cloaks the whispers,
In the dark, haikus take shape,
Shadows weave their chant.

Silent stories told,
Etched in the air, stark and bold,
Haikus find their home.

Murmurs in the gloom,
Words tailored by the night's loom,
Poetry in bloom.

Unvoiced Lyricism Bound

In the kingdom of the mute and the mild,
Unspoken lyrics, tender and wild,
Rhythms deeply bound in silence's hold,
Harmony unheard, stories untold.

Melodies hummed in a quiet breath,
A symphony held in a silent death,
Soft whispers of a heart unrefined,
Unvoiced lyricism entwined.

Echos of sentiments, quietly caged,
Emotions on the stanza, neatly paged,
Hush of the depths, under restraint,
Bound lyricism, an unsung saint.

Sub rosa Scrolls Transcribed

Beneath the veil of the rose's scent,
Scripts transcribe the esoteric bent,
Sub rosa stories, old and wise,
Tales that from the deepest roots arise.

Each scroll a keeper of the arcane,
Words whispered, not in vain,
Secret scripts, a hidden trove,
Lines where silent oaths rove.

Written under the shroud of mystery,
Scrolls hold the keys to history,
Sub rosa knowledge, in quiet script,
Through hidden lines, the truth is slipped.

Vows Veiled in Verse

Upon the altar of whispered breeze,
The oaths we cloak in twilight's shroud,
Words woven with the silk of seas,
Our silent vows declared aloud.

In the cadence of rustling leaves,
Echoes the promise of our youth,
Underneath the starry eves,
We speak in rhymes that mask the truth.

Hands clasped tight in harmony,
We dance to the music of our dream,
Each motion tells the story,
Of love’s endless, flowing stream.

In the hush before the morning,
Verses hold our bond so tight,
Within the dawn's soft warning,
We are one in fading night.

Soliloquies of Secrecy

In the mirror, I confide,
Glimpses of the self I hide,
Secrets in my heart reside,
Silent whispers locked inside.

Dialogues with my own soul,
Speaking parts of me I stole,
Shrouded thoughts I can't control,
In the depths of my hidden role.

To the night, I bare my core,
Inner stage of silent war,
Lines recited evermore,
In the solace of closed doors.

Veiled beneath the moon's soft glow,
Soliloquies in whispers low,
No other soul will ever know,
The secrecy my heart does stow.

Whispered Truths on Paper

With pen in hand I dare to write,
The silent truths that shun the light,
On paper plains they take their flight,
As whispered words become my kite.

Unspoken dreams in ink I trust,
Bearing secrets like autumn's gust,
To the page, my raw thoughts thrust,
In parchment confide, I must.

Through the veins of every letter,
Speak the soul’s unchained fetter,
Written bonds that feel much better,
Than silent weight of life’s debtor.

In each curve and line I pour,
Truths that gently open the door,
My heart's voice, forevermore,
In written whispers, it will soar.

Clandestine Confessions in Ink

Beneath the quill of moonlit hue,
The deepest confessions quietly brew,
Tracing secrets, old and new,
Ink tells what I dare not view.

Each drop spills forth from the heart's crypt,
Wording a legacy, line encrypted,
Feelings in parchment, carefully scripted,
Under the silence, truth is depicted.

Whisper to paper, a discreet affair,
Textual echoes of a soul laid bare,
Revelations cloaked with care,
Ink and thought in secret prayer.

Lines intertwine, truth's tapestry,
Artful renditions of what cannot be,
Clandestine tales set free,
Confesiones etched for none to see.

Cadence of the Cryptic

In shadows where the whispers dwell,
A cryptic dance, a silent spell,
Beneath the moon's covert glance,
Mysteries weave an intricate trance.

An enigma wrapped in the night,
With secrets cloaked from mortal sight,
Every turn, a hidden plea,
A ballet of the arcane and free.

A rhythm known to the arcane,
Where silence speaks and shadows reign,
Each motion tells what words can't say,
In the cadence of the cryptic ballet.

This ritual old, as time itself,
A tome of wisdom—not for the shelf,
Through gestures known to ancient sects,
Lies a lore that time protects.

Unheard Echoes in Script

On parchment bare, the unseen words,
Unheard echoes, like flightless birds,
They resonate within the soul,
A script where silent tales unroll.

Forgotten whispers of the pen,
That speak the thoughts beyond our ken,
In hollow halls of thoughts interned,
Lie messages that were never learned.

Each stroke holds a mute refrain,
A secret life in ink-stained vein,
Captured within the lines, a plea,
For eyes to read, for hearts to see.

Scripts of silence, boundless, deep,
In every curve, mysteries seep,
Though silent, their intent is scripted clear,
Unheard echoes anyone can hear.

Epistles of the Esoteric

To seekers of the veiled truth,
These epistles hold the vermouth,
Encrypted with an age-old key,
That unlocks the esoteric spree.

Pages filled with ancient lore,
In symbols strange forevermore,
Invite the mind to wander through,
Realms concealed from public view.

Every line a hidden door,
Into a world not seen before,
Letters form with purpose cryptic,
Narratives esoterically mystic.

These sacred texts, kept from the light,
Preserve their knowledge through the night,
For those who read with inner sight,
Find the path that leads to the arcane height.

Sonnets of Subterfuge

In veils of verse and rhyme disguise,
Sonnets cloak their cunning lies,
Beneath the beauty of the phrase,
Dwell secrets veiled in foggy haze.

Each line a ruse, a hidden snare,
Poetic whispers fill the air,
A deft deception dressed in art,
Designed to play upon the heart.

Within the cadence, schemes unfold,
As stories not quite true are told,
Beneath the guise of meter tight,
Dwells duplicity out of sight.

Secure within the crafted scenes,
Subterfuge in structured means,
Through verses of intended drift,
Ensnares the mind with silent shift.

Undisclosed Sonnets Created

In whispers soft, where shadows dance,
Along the walls, with furtive glance,
Unseen the quill does fly and prance,
Undisclosed sonnets here, perchance.

Within the heart's secluded halls,
Where silence sings and echo calls,
Each stanza climbs and never falls,
The muse entwines its secret thralls.

The words are born from deepest care,
Not shown nor known, just silent prayer,
Veiled under the cloak of air,
Within the mind's own quiet lair.

These verses hold, in tight embrace,
The sentiments that time won't chase,
Carefully filed in memory's space,
Undisclosed sonnets find their place.

Hidden Dispatches Noted

Beneath the moon’s discreet caress,
Secrets stir in soft duress,
Notes once hidden now address,
The heart's clandestine game of chess.

Each line a code, a covert spate,
Whispered leaves that will not wait,
Convey messages innate,
From sealed lips that separate.

Scripts tucked away, in shadows they hide,
Masked intentions, side by side,
Years may pass, yet still abide,
Hidden dispatches, noted with pride.

Silent ink spells out the lore,
Of all those thoughts kept at the core,
Through quiet dispatches they outpour,
The unspoken dreams that they store.

Disguised Lullabies Emoted

Rocking gently in night's cloak,
Tales unsung and words unspoke,
The lullabies we wove, evoke,
A tranquil guise that dreams provoke.

Humming tunes of tender verse,
Enveloped by the universe,
Each note a masked, silent curse,
In disguise, emotions disperse.

Crooned beneath the vigilant stars,
Carrying hopes that might be ours,
Past the sting of life's raw scars,
Disguised lullabies reach afar.

Serenading the hearts that dote,
On every softly emoted note,
In dreams, we drift, together afloat,
In the night, these lullabies coat.

Veiled Sentiments Scribbled

With every stroke of pen on paper,
The heart does spill where none can taper,
Veiled sentiments begin to caper,
Shrouded words form a quiet draper.

Each scribbled line, a hidden plea,
From shackles of silence, longs to flee,
In code they're clothed, so none can see,
The whispers of the heart's decree.

Through ink, the silent speak is heard,
Couched in metaphor and word,
The heart's true essence softly stirred,
Its cryptic truth remains interred.

Behold the script where feelings swivel,
Where every curve and dot is civil,
Yet under wraps, emotions shrivel,
In veiled sentiments, thoughts unravel.

Palimpsest of Forbidden Words

In whispers hollowed out, they lay so still,
Engraved in layers, time cannot decay,
A tome of thoughts the world would often kill,
Yet secrets speak where silence holds its sway.

Remnants of verses once kissed by the sun,
Now muted murmurs of the heart's desire,
Dusky desires, into the ether spun,
Ink bleeds through histories, igniting fire.

Each faded line, a story to unfurl,
A script obscured by newer tales imposed,
The past a ghost, its narrative to curl,
In whispers, truths of ancients are disclosed.

Hear the chorus beneath the etched out lies,
Where censored spirits in defiance rise.

Unraveled Yarns of Yesterday

Worn threads of memory, gently teased apart,
The fabric of the past, a tapestry,
In and out the labyrinth of the heart,
Weaving the yarns of what used to be.

Frayed at the ends where time has had its chew,
Colored with shades of laughter and of tears,
Knots of moments, love once thought true,
All intertwined through the passing years.

Fingers trace the patterns, now undone,
Each twist and loop a day that slipped away,
In unraveling, the end is spun,
And yet within each thread, the colors stay.

For in unwinding tales of yesterday,
A quiet wisdom threads its silent way.

Echoes of Erased Epiphanies

Hollow halls where once bright revelations rang,
Soft footfalls stir the silence into sound,
In shadows, muted voices once that sang,
Their whispered wisdom in the darkness bound.

The mind's eye blinks at truths it used to hold,
Ephemeral, like dew at morning's touch,
As time's erasure turns the new to old,
The echoed wisdom doesn't echo much.

Yet in the quiet corners of the mind,
The remnants of epiphanies persist,
Though mute and muffled, seek and ye shall find,
The ghosts of thoughts the censor's hand has missed.

For in the echoes of the mind's retreats,
Lie dormant seeds of once profound conceits.

Balladry of the Barricaded

Behind the walls of will, the heart does pound,
The silent sonnets sung to stones unhearing,
In fortification, feelings wrapped around,
The balladry of souls, the brave endearing.

Each verse a brick, each rhyme a rugged stone,
Creating ramparts high to fight the night,
Within the chest, the rhythm beats alone,
The barricaded ballads holding tight.

But through the cracks, the melodies may bleed,
The songs of sorrow and of joy entwine,
A fugue of fortitude in times of need,
The harmonies of hidden hearts align.

For even caged in walls, the spirit sings,
And from the depth, a quiet courage brings.

Whispers on Parchment

In silent halls where shadows play,
A quill dances the night away.
Words like soft hums in dimming light,
Secrets told to the parchment white.

Each letter a sigh, a confession,
An intimate, silent procession.
The ink trails off, a whispered lore,
A silent script, a myth of yore.

The echoes of the murmured past,
In scripted lines, forever cast.
Whispers cling to the fibrous page,
A timeless act upon life's stage.

In the still air, the words entwine,
A tapestry of thoughts benign.
Soft murmurs pressed in sheets refine,
Where silence speaks and souls align.

Clandestine Verses

Behind the shroud of night so deep,
Where shadows stir and vigils keep.
Subtle words entwined, fates rehearse,
In clandestine verses, terse.

A covert dance of ink and will,
Hidden codes that thrills instill.
Loose lips may sink ships unforeseen,
In the quiet, a subtle glean.

Whispered rhymes of secret trysts,
Delicacies in the mist.
Entangled tales of the unknown,
Bound in lines intricately sewn.

They speak in tongues of the arcane,
In hushed refrains that shall remain.
Across the quiet, night construes,
In verses veiled, the hidden clues.

Ink of the Unspoken

Upon the canvas, stark and bare,
Ink spills secrets it dares not share.
The unspoken words, a liquid dance,
Captured in silence, given a chance.

A torrent of thoughts, unvoiced, unheard,
Flows from the nib, word by measured word.
An undercurrent of mute desires,
Set alight, an ember that never tires.

This ink, the herald of hearts unmet,
The silent discourse of a sun long set.
A lexicon of longing, neatly penned,
In glyphs that whisper, softly mend.

It paints the dreams we dare not speak,
In hues of hope, for the strong, the weak.
The paper holds, in its veiny grip,
The unspoken journey of a soul's trip.

Hushed Stanzas

In the realm where quiet reigns,
Stand verses wrought in silent strains.
They hold the breath of the subdued,
Elegies to the solitude.

The metered lines, a quiet pact,
With every pause subtly intact.
Hushed stanzas with no sound to chase,
Each word a gentle, soft embrace.

The sentiments that dare not roar,
Are whispered through the poet's lore.
In muted hues, the stanza's plea,
A tender, silent symphony.

With tender touch, the whispering quill,
Writes the souls wish, the heart's still.
In the hush, the verses nest,
Within the stanza’s quiet behest.

Codex of the Covert

In halls of whispering steel and stone,
A codex lies with words unknown.
Secrets draped in shadows' veil,
A silent language tells its tale.

Within the pages, ink runs deep,
A legacy the covert keep.
Encrypted lore at midnight's call,
Scribes the truth, unseen by all.

Guardians of the silent script,
Through time's tight grip, it's deftly slipped.
Woven into the darkened night,
Their silent stories dodge the light.

Ballads of the Buried

Beneath the earth in restful beds,
The past whispers its long-lost threads.
Songs of the buried, soft and low,
In the silence, their stories grow.

Echoes of days and dreams entwined,
Where fate and destiny unaligned.
In every ballad, truth conferred,
In every silence, history heard.

So listen close to ground's soft moan,
Where seeds of bygone eras sewn.
Their ballads haunt the patient ear,
Each note a secret held so dear.

Scripted Shadows

In the gloom, the quills dance fast,
Scripted shadows in the past.
Lines of darkness scrawled on walls,
Tell the tales that nightfall calls.

Through the ink, a story's birth,
Spanning wide across the Earth.
Shadowy chronicles set free,
An eternal mystery to see.

Fleeting silhouettes entwined,
In the parchment of the mind.
Scribing secrets, lost, unnamed,
In the dim, our thoughts are framed.

Unveiled by Quill

The quill glides and truths reveal,
A world unseen begins to heal.
Words once cloaked in enigma's shroud,
Now speak their wisdom clear and loud.

Unveiled by quill, the once occult,
Becomes a key, a lock, an exalt.
With every stroke, a vision decries,
The shrouded world before our eyes.

So may the quill forever spill,
The tales of all who wish and will.
In silent ink, let truth be found,
By quill's work, let secrets be unbound.

Whispers Among Lines

In hushed tones the paper speaks,
A silent symphony in sheets.
Each letter dances, bold and fine,
On the stage of the whispered lines.

Gossamer words in twilight's embrace,
Speak secrets, hidden without a trace.
Verse to verse in clandestine meets,
Confessions soft as evening retreats.

The murmur of ink, a gentle sigh,
As tales unfold 'neath moonlit sky.
Fleeting thoughts in tandem twine,
A lovers' dance, serpentine.

So listen close to the silent hymns,
In the quietude, understanding swims.
Among the lines, wisdom decrees,
In every whisper, a soul breathes.

Threads of Concealed Thought

Threads of thought, finely spun,
Weave the essence of the quietly undone.
In mindscape's loom, they twist and sway,
Concealing notions in the fray.

Woven secrets in the tapestry of mind,
Seek the seams that which to unbind.
Silken lines threading through the heart,
Hidden wisdom they quietly impart.

Through the maze of the unsaid word,
Quiet thoughts wait to be heard.
In the stillness, hear the mental fraught,
Within the threads of concealed thought.

Shrouded mysteries' tender plot,
Weave the yarn that time forgot.
Let the mind's spool delicately wrought,
Unravel the threads of concealed thought.

Dreamscapes of the Dormant

In the theater of the serenely still,
Slumber's brush paints at will.
Landscapes born of the deepest sleep,
Where dreams may soar, and dive deep.

A thousand colors in the mind's eye,
Morphing shapes in the dusk's sigh.
Through valleys lush and mountains steep,
Dreamers wander, in their sleep.

In the tapestry of night's embrace,
Each thread a path, interlaced.
As serenity's hand guides fate's oar,
To shores of the ever-dormant lore.

The quill of slumber, dipped in night,
Scripts the tales that take flight.
Silent whispers in every form,
Weave the dreamscapes of the dormant.

Notations of the Night

The night in its splendor, a silent score,
Stars above, like notes to adore.
Each twinkle a beat in the celestial sight,
A symphony crafted in the arms of night.

Luna's glow, a gentle lead,
Pens nocturnes where darkness recedes.
The quiet earth listens, still and tight,
As the heavens play the notations of the night.

Through zephyrs that hum and sway the trees,
The rustling leaves perform with ease.
Crickets chime in, to add their light,
Harmonizing the notations of the night.

So let the cosmos's music embark,
On a journey through the ethereal dark.
With every melody, it does invite,
One to savor the notations of the night.

Inmost Rhymes Penned

Within the caverns of the soul, so deep,
In shadows where my quiet secrets keep,
Ink bleeds upon the page, a silent cry,
Each word a whisper of my inner sky.

Two halves converse where none can intercede,
The heart and mind in an eternal creed,
Penned down the essence of my silent hymn,
The inmost rhymes that swirl 'neath surface dim.

Lines intertwine like roots beneath the soil,
Narrating tales of inner toil and spoil,
Crafted in the alcoves of my domain,
The parchment holds what time cannot constrain.

This script is mine alone, a sacred rite,
With verses veiled in dusk and candlelight,
The pen, it dances to a quiet tune,
The inmost rhymes are sung beneath the moon.

Covert Idylls Imagined

In dreamscape's fold, I find my secret glade,
Where thoughts like wildflowers in the sun parade,
A covert idyll wrought of mind's desire,
Is kindled softly by the heart's own fire.

Each petal blooms in colors yet unnamed,
In whispered breezes, fantasy's proclaimed,
These secret gardens grow from fertile ground,
Here in imagination's depth, unbound.

A stream of consciousness that softly flows,
It carves its path wherever fancy goes,
Reflecting hopes and fears that seldom speak,
Upon these hidden banks, they find their peak.

Enclosed within the mind's secluded maze,
Imagined idylls live in private blaze,
Structures of calm built far from prying eyes,
A covert sanctuary from life's disguise.

Inner Dialogues Profiled

The soliloquy within prattles on,
A ceaseless dialogue from dusk till dawn,
Profiles of questions with their answers dance,
In corridors of self, a silent trance.

Two facets of the self in deep debate,
With inner voices that articulate,
The essence of my being put to test,
In chambers where my doubts take little rest.

Versed echoes bouncing off the mental walls,
Each whispering shadow rises and falls,
Such dialogues that craft my inner lore,
Retelling myths my spirit did explore.

Here lies the plot of mind's internal strife,
A narrative that weaves through threads of life,
Profiles inscribed in intellect's own hand,
Inner dialogues that understand their stand.

Unearthed Sophistries Structured

Beneath a veil of rhetoric so plain,
Lies structured sophistry, a mind's terrain,
Unearthed, each argument gains shape and form,
In sophist's craft, the norm is to transform.

With structured artifice of clever speech,
Defending notions just beyond one's reach,
The wiles of logic twist, turn, and entwine,
Concealing faults within a polished shine.

Artful the words that snake through every clause,
Beneath their elegance, a slighted cause,
Yet still they rise, these edifices bold,
The structured sophistries that truth withhold.

An architect of argument's design,
Where reason's threads through fallacy entwine,
In every crafted phrase, intent is masked,
Sophistries unearthed, in rhetoric basked.

Shrouded Memoirs Composed

In twilight's gentle sighs, memories brew,
A tapestry of thoughts, so faint, so true.
Each thread a tale, a whispered past embrace,
In the quietude, old dreams interlace.

Forgotten yesterdays in shadows dance,
Time's subtle thieves that steal away by chance.
Yet in this hush, these veiled remembrances soar,
Shrouded memoirs composed, alive once more.

Gentle they rise on night's embracing breeze,
Carrying secrets wrapped in mysteries.
In the silence, they hum a tune so old,
The melody of stories left untold.

Softly they linger in the calm, dark night,
Echoes of a life just beyond the light.
In the stillness, they leave their silent mark,
A glowing ember in the endless dark.

Cryptic Scripts Unfolded

Ancient scripts, a language lost in time,
Carefully unfurled, a rhythm, a rhyme.
Symbols etched in dust, carved ages ago,
Cryptic messages from the long shadow.

Ink-stained fingers trace the curves and lines,
Deciphering the past, where truth entwines.
Each letter unfolds history's tight clasp,
Whispers of a world within a grasp.

Mysteries concealed in folds of old scroll,
Unlocking the secrets, fulfilling the role.
Translating silence that once was word,
Giving voice to stories unheard.

Pages weathered by the toils of time,
Revealing epochs in an endless climb.
Enigmas no longer enfolded in sleep,
Through cryptic scripts, into the present they leap.

Covert Letters Aligned

Beneath a veil of secrecy, they find,
Covert letters aligned, bound and intertwined.
Subtle in expression, hidden in script,
Keys to a narrative, long ago slipped.

In cryptic alphabets, meanings concealed,
Waiting for the moment to be revealed.
A clandestine dance of shadows and light,
Where silent characters jump into sight.

Secrets penned in quiet subversion,
Across time and space, a secret conversation.
Symbols that engage in covert discourse,
A silent language setting the unseen course.

Quietly they gather in rows so refined,
Legacy encoded, yet designed to remind.
The lore and the whisper of history's flight,
Through covert letters aligned just right.

Encrypted Stanzas Revealed

Within the cypher of the moon's soft glow,
Encrypted stanzas revealed for those who know.
A coded ballet spinning the night away,
Where letters pirouette, then slyly sway.

Each verse a lock, each rhyme a silver key,
Unlocking dreams that float on a silent sea.
Stanzas of mist, in the air they confide,
Secrets not broken, but trustingly supplied.

Words that are hidden beneath the surface tide,
Waiting for the insight, to open wide.
A treasure trove of lore, in metaphor sealed,
Now decrypted gently, meaning is revealed.

Veiled poetry now shedding its disguise,
A cascade of truths under starry skies.
Once unknown, now familiar in its feel,
In the softest whisper, encrypted stanzas revealed.

Chiffonier Rhymes Collected

In wooden veins, the secrets dwell,
Drawer by drawer, a story fell.
Whispers of linen, the chiffonier's charm,
Echoes of treasures, keeping them from harm.

Curved legs of pine, in dim-lit room,
Where cobwebs dance and memories bloom.
Each knob a verse, a poet's dream,
Dusty sonnets, an antique theme.

Socks and letters, fragments of lives,
Hidden in corners where sentiment thrives.
A cabinet of verses, rhymes well kept,
The tales of the ages, in woodwork adept.

It stands alone, a silent ode,
A symphony in grain, in the shadows' abode.
Rhymes collected, stories stored,
The chiffonier whispers, its lore unexplored.

Silhouettes of Syntax Arranged

Upon a page, the shadows play,
Sentences dance as light fades away.
In twilight's ink, the words align,
Silhouettes of syntax, a poetic design.

Curved letters cast their somber spell,
Tales take shape, in the quiet swell.
Phrases flicker, a choreographed light,
Illuminating the prose of the coming night.

Each paragraph, a silhouette obscure,
The structured verse holds meaning pure.
In rhythm's embrace, the story's arranged,
By the flicker of candle, the context changed.

The darkened contours of letters' flight,
Bound within the borders of dwindling light.
In the opaque dance of ink and theme,
Arranged, is the syntax in the writer's dream.

Uncharted Sonnets Pieced

Beyond the maps of known refrain,
Lie sonnets wild, untamed terrain.
Where words are wind and thoughts take sail,
Uncharted verses on the poetic trail.

In the expanse of unbound script,
New rhythms form, and rhyme is clipped.
Stanzas like islands dot the rhyme,
The poet's compass, turning with time.

Each line a longitude of soul's desire,
Each metaphor, a latitude higher.
In the sea of parchment, the ink runs deep,
Sonnets pieced from the silent heap.

Navigate the heart's vast sea,
Find the treasure of verse to be.
With pen as anchor, draft sublime,
In the scrolls uncharted, let the sonnets climb.

Implicit Vignettes Wrought

In crafted words, the subtext weaves,
In between lines, where meaning cleaves.
Implicit vignettes in sentences caught,
A tapestry of nuance thoughtfully wrought.

A whisper here, a glance there told,
Narratives silent, yet stories bold.
The spaces filled with readers' sight,
Exchange of wisdom, veiled in light.

Glimpses of life's intimate plays,
Moments captured in hidden ways.
Skillful hands shape text unseen,
Where the lines end, and insights glean.

The unspoken heart of tales is sought,
In quietude, the deepest lessons taught.
Between the written, the artist's draught,
In subtlety, the vignettes are wrought.

Legacies Left in Lines

Whispers of wisdom etched in age,
Ancestral voices fill the stage.
Lines of life, of love, of lore,
Legacies that forever soar.

Through gentle brush or sculptor's hands,
Echoes pervade through time's vast sands.
The written word, a force so fine,
A tapestry where souls entwine.

Pages yellowed, edges frayed,
Yet in their hearts, the truths arrayed.
Legacies that withstand the tides,
In written lines, where hope abides.

Scribbled in corners of history's halls,
In silent strength the spirit calls.
Ink that flows from pens long still,
Leaves a legacy, a timeless quill.

Tales Told in Trust

Around the fires, beneath the moon,
Stories whirl in a mystic tune.
Tales told softly, in hushed embrace,
In trust they bond, time cannot erase.

Lessons of valor, of love, of fears,
Secrets carried through the years.
In trust, these stories find their keep,
In every heart, they're sown deep.

Elders speak in voices just,
Every whisper wrapped in trust.
Children listen, eyes so wide,
In these tales, their dreams reside.

Within the circle, truth is shared,
A sacred space, where souls are bared.
In trust, the lineage of lore,
Tales that live forevermore.

Memoirs of the Mysterious

Hidden beneath the cloak of night,
Mysteries veiled from plainest sight.
Memoirs inscribed on ancient stones,
Secrets residing in hallowed bones.

Tales of whispers, actions veiled,
Where common eyes have always failed.
Bound by silence, kept apart,
Memoirs written in the dark.

In the shadows, they conspire,
The unknown fuels the curious fire.
In the deep, their stories rest,
Mysterious lives, unconfessed.

Chapters closed to the day's light,
Bearing wisdom of the night.
Memoirs kept from prying eyes,
In mystery, the truth lies.

Forbidden Phrases

Words of power, locked away,
Forbidden phrases we dare not say.
The tongue, a key to doors unseen,
Unlocking realms where few have been.

Echoes of the ancient spell,
Within the silence, secrets dwell.
Whispers of what must not be heard,
In every hushed and sacred word.

Silent guardians keep the code,
Along the path less often strode.
Phrases that can break the chains,
The weight of silence, it remains.

Speak not the words that stir the air,
Unleashing forces, raw and bare.
Forbidden phrases bide their time,
In silence wrapped, they dwell sublime.

Esoteric Idioms Framed

In whispered tongues, the sages muse,
Across the age-old canvas spread.
The idioms cryptic, they infuse,
With meanings rich, but rarely read.

Veiled phrases dance with shadows twined,
Beneath the alcove's dim-lit charm.
Each word a key, for minds refined,
To open doors of thought, disarm.

Fragments of wisdom, lost to time,
In vellum books, they gently sleep.
Awakened line by cryptic line,
Where seekers delve, profoundly deep.

A tapestry of thought unveiled,
With threads of mystery inlaid.
In esoteric terms assailed,
The idioms stand, timelessly sprayed.

Undertones of Intimacy

Whispers soft as silk on skin,
Quiet laughter in the hush.
Eyes that speak of love's begin,
And hearts in gentle, rhythmic rush.

Touches light as falling leaves,
In the glow of fading light.
How the tangled soul believes,
In the truth found in the night.

Breath to breath, a silent song,
Lips unspoken words inspire.
In this place, where none belong,
Save for two, alight with fire.

Candle's shadow on the wall,
Dances with our every move.
Undertones that sweetly call,
In the intimacy's groove.

Unrevealed Desires Stroked

Beneath the veil of twilight gaze,
Where secret hopes begin to wake.
The yearnings of the heart's soft maze,
As whispers of desire partake.

Unseen, the wishes kept at bay,
Caressed by moonlight's tender stroke.
In dreams where night outlasts the day,
And passion's breath is gently spoke.

The touch of longing's secret hand,
That guides the soul through mists of fire.
Each motion under its command,
To stroke the chords of deep desire.

In the hallowed halls of thought,
Where fervent wishes dance and twirl.
The unrevealed is sought,
And stroked to life as desires unfurl.

Axioms of the Absent

Silent echos call the lost,
In the language of the void.
Unwritten codes at such a cost,
Where emptiness is best enjoyed.

Absent truths that linger near,
In the corners of our eye.
Glimpses of the far, so clear,
In the vastness of the sky.

The laws of none, a paradox,
Spoken in the language rare.
As time unwinds the ancient clocks,
And leaves the axioms bare.

Seek what's not, find what you will,
In the tranquil sea's absent wave.
The quiet space, where time stands still,
And wisdom whispers from beyond the grave.

Unfolding Private Myths

In twilight's hush, a silent call,
Whispered secrets start to thrall,
Ancestral tales on winds do sigh,
As stars peep from the ink-black sky.

Within the mind's deep, arcane crypts,
Private myths start to eclipse,
The known, the absolute, the sure,
New sagas form in contours pure.

With every heart's clandestine beat,
Old legends rise, new epochs greet,
Shadows dance to an inner theme,
While reveling in a moonbeam's gleam.

Our inner worlds do twist and fold,
Narratives bold, quietly told,
On parchment of the soul they're inked,
In chambers where the dragons blinked.

Under Wraps Rhymes

Rhymes that lounge in shadows deep,
Where murmurs dwell and willows weep,
Under wraps of time and space,
Speak in tones with subtle grace.

Verses veiled in mystery's cloak,
Escaping from the minds they soak,
Crafted neath the silent moon,
Humming an ancient, wordless tune.

Whispered in the dead of night,
Beneath the waning candlelight,
Couplets enshrined in hidden nooks,
Unveiling worlds in secret books.

Under wraps, these rhymes persist,
In the mists of the unkissed,
They conjure imagery so rife,
Weaving the threads of quieter life.

Articulations of the Averted

Eyes that flicker, then divert,
Words unspoken, subtly curt,
Lines of verse that swerve and sway,
Telling tales of yesterday.

Silent musings softly tread,
O'er the matters never said,
Cautiously they paint the air,
With strokes of things that aren't there.

Veiled expressions, gestures slight,
Hide the day's reluctant light,
Articulate in silence deep,
Revelations that we keep.

Moments glossed, turned aside,
In articulations, they abide,
Fleeting shadows softly part,
Uttering the averted heart.

Intimations in the Margins

In the margins, whispers bide,
Casting certainty aside,
Intimations softly creep,
Where the ink begins to seep.

Gentle hints among the lines,
Where the boundary reclines,
Suggestive of a deeper hue,
Offering a hidden clue.

Margins bear the secret signs,
Of wayward thoughts and redesigns,
Making room for silent speech,
Just beyond the center's reach.

Notes that linger off the edge,
Binding truth with a subtle pledge,
In every quiet nook they start,
Hinting at the artist's heart.

Undercover Elegies Expressed

In the silence of the undercover night,
Veils of sorrow lightly rest,
Elegies whispered under moonlight's crest,
Echoes of love's tender, forlorn plight.

Hidden pains within the stars' bright gaze,
Trail of tears in the sky's vast seas,
Silent laments carried by the breeze,
Mourning dreams that the dark tends to raze.

Cloaked in shadows, heartaches dare not speak,
Yet their presence is ever so strong,
In the silence, we learn to belong,
To the secret sorrows that we seek.

Every ending that time compels,
In an elegy's embrace, it swells,
Softly sung by the night's covert quells,
Undercover, where true feeling dwells.

Innermost Echoes Inscribed

Upon the parchment of my soul, inscribed,
Secret whispers, my innermost echoes,
In each line, a hidden truth encloses,
Feelings deep that I have long prescribed.

Words that stem from the well of my heart,
Bearing essence of all that's unspoken,
Bound by silence, yet never broken,
Inscribed echoes that never depart.

Scripted in the ink of introspection,
Each echo with its own tone and hue,
Capturing what I hold to be true,
A manuscript of intimate connection.

Between the lines, a quiet revelation,
Echoes penned with silent contemplation,
In each verse, an earnest stipulation,
A soul's dialogue in tranquil translation.

Taciturn Versifications Projected

Projected on life’s indifferent screen,
The poems of the taciturn, unsaid,
Quiet tales of joy and of dread,
Reading between the lines unseen.

Words are cast like shadows on the wall,
Forming verses from the mute's discourse,
In their silence, a resonant force,
Speaking loudly as they softly fall.

In the quiet, their power is found,
The taciturn's script, profoundly sound,
Writing worlds where thoughts are unbound,
Versifications in silence crowned.

A projection of the voiceless heart,
Where sentiments play the starring part,
Poetry's power, a silent art,
In each mute verse, expression's start.

Unexposed Prose Envisioned

In mindscape's hidden, tranquil field,
Lies the unexposed prose, quietly sealed,
A garden of words yet to be revealed,
Visions in the heart still concealed.

Sentences form beneath the veil,
Truths that the lips dare not tell,
Stories await with their own spell,
In the mind's eye where they dwell.

Envisioned worlds rich with lore,
Prose unspoken touches the core,
A secret script of the nevermore,
Hidden meanings ready to explore.

Within the quiet, imagined scene,
Narratives woven from the unseen,
Prose that dreams in silence, serene,
In the unexposed, beauty is keen.

Confiding in Cursive

In looped letters, my truths gently twine
Cursive whispers of thoughts so divine
Each curve bears a secret, in ink it does purse
Betwixt lines of beauty, my confidence immerses

Silent motions that dance and converse
Tales of the heart, in script they immerse
Flowing like rivers through canyons of paper
Letters entwined, a textual draper

Scripted confessions, not one is the same
In elegant scrolls, I sign my name
Emotions emboldened, in loops and in swirls
A cursive confession, to unfurl

In this timeless dance, my pen won't reverse
For only in cursive, my soul can transverse
With each stroke and flourish, I'm softly assured
My silent musings are safely secured

Sentinels of the Subtext

Beneath the lines, the sentinels stand
Guarding the meaning where the implications land
Their silent forms between the gaps reside
In the subtext, they silently guide

They watch and wait in the white unseen
Understanding born in the spaces between
With each word that's written, and those left out
They keep the secrets that words may doubt

Unspoken guards of the quiet intent
They know the message that was truly meant
In the echo of what is not said aloud
Lies the truth that's wrapped in a shroud

Sentinels solemn, with duty so grave
Bearing the burden of the messages they save
In the realm of meaning where they exact
Stand the vigilant watchmen of the subtext

Revelations in Erasure

Words once bold, now ghosts on the page
Erased from existence, from the textual stage
In the absence of letters, new meanings arise
Truths unfold in a silent surprise

With each stroke that diminishes the phrase
Emerges a clarity from the erasing haze
What's left unsaid speaks volumes more
Than words that in ink once confidently wore

Spaces and blanks now tell the tale
Of what once was scribed, now faint and pale
A revelation in each vanished line
A story reborn, a redefined design

So within this parchment, a paradox lies
Where the erased whispers, and the silence sighs
In erasures, we find the core essence pure
As it reveals a narrative obscure

Metaphors for the Muted

Silent souls speak in symbols so clear
In metaphors, the muted draw near
With veiled voices, their stories unfold
In imagery bold, their silence is told

Each likeness a lifeline thrown to the deep
A language for secrets that they keep
In allegories, they find their release
An artistic expression, a silent peace

For those who listen with more than their ears
Will hear the muted, despite their fears
Their indirect speech, a resplendent array
Of lives lived loudly, in a quiet display

So heed the metaphors, the silent cries
In cloaked communication, truth never dies
For even when words are softly muted
In poetic semblance, they're astutely suited

Mystic Messages Doodled

In twilight's embrace, the shadows commune,
Whispering secrets to the crescent moon.
The stars overhead in silent accord,
Doodle mystic messages on night's blackboard.

Veiled in the dark, soft murmurs arise,
A symphony scripted in the skies.
Each flickering light, a celestial phrase,
Encoded in the universe's maze.

A language so ancient, etched in the ether,
Sailing on cosmos, light as a feather.
Hope's constellation, love's gentle guide,
Cast on the canvas of night, far and wide.

Through time's fabric, the constellations drift,
In eternal dance, they twist and they sift.
Within their embrace, enigmas are spun,
Until the arrival of the telling sun.

Camouflaged Quatrains Arranged

Nature's palette blends in quiet disguise,
The hidden verses in plain sight arise.
Camouflaged lines amongst leaves and dirt,
Invisibly scribed in the earth, they flirt.

Barren trees whisper in rustling refrain,
Their quatrains arranged by the wind's campaign.
As creatures inch forth with silent footfall,
They heed the call, through the thrall, of the wild's install.

Beneath the underbrush, a furtive script,
There, truths of life are cleverly crypt.
Each branch a quatrain, each bloom a verse,
In camouflaged odes, nature's stories disperse.

In the forest depths where the light's deranged,
The messages lie, camouflaged, exchanged.
Nature's pen writes on, without need for praise,
In its hidden quatrains, life unfurls and plays.

Furtive Odes Conceived

In the quiet nook of the unbidden thought,
Where furtive odes are secretly wrought,
Ideas that dance in the shadows of mind,
Hidden from view, in the silence, confined.

In whispers of the heart, softly they're penned,
Furtive and shy, to none do they lend.
Fearing the starkness of daylight's reveal,
In the dark recess, they cautiously wheel.

With each beat and rhythm, covertly fetched,
These worded treasures are silently etched.
Conceived in the hush of a sole reverie,
Guarded and cloaked in earnest brevity.

Yet, in the ink of the night, they emerge,
From the depths of stillness, they quietly surge.
Furtive odes written with the faintest light,
Await the brave moment to come into sight.

Surreal Musings Recorded

Draped in the fabric of dreams, thoughts entwine,
Where reality and fantasy dance and align.
The impossible, in ink, with grace is bestowed,
Surreal musings in silent verses flowed.

Upon the canvas of slumber, shades paint,
Each stroke casts a world without restraint.
With every hue, the surreal takes form,
In the tranquil chaos, new realities are born.

Through mists of the mind, with gentle trace,
Impossible truths find their resting place.
Recorded in rhyme, outside time's command,
They spiral and twirl, a curious wonderland.

These are the poems from dream's deep reservoir,
Whispering tales of lands both near and far.
In the tapestry of sleep, each word is sown,
Where the seeds of the surreal are faithfully grown.

Printed in the USA
CPSIA information can be obtained
at www.ICGtesting.com
LVHW081241021223
765302LV00010B/157

9 789916 394649